MY INCREDIBLE RAINFOREST EXPEDITION

Written by Susan Mayes
Illustrated by Emma Martinez

Top That Publishing
Tide Mill Way, Woodbridge, Suffolk, IP12 1AP, UK
www.imaginethat.com
Top That is an imprint of Imagine That Group Ltd
Copyright © 2023 Imagine That Group Ltd
EU Authorised Representative, Vulcan Consulting,
38/39 Fitzwilliam Square West, Dublin 2, D02 NX53, Ireland
All rights reserved
0 2 4 6 8 9 7 5 3 1
Manufactured in Guangdong, China

WELCOME TO THE RAINFOREST

Your incredible rainforest expedition starts here! With this explorer's fact book and the model in your kit, you have special access to the amazing world of rainforest wildlife. This is your pass to becoming a top explorer and a rainforest expert!

WHAT IS A RAINFOREST?

A rainforest is a **thick forest of tall trees and vegetation** found in tropical areas of the world, near the equator — an imaginary line around the middle of the Earth. These areas have **lots of heat and rain**, which make perfect growing conditions for plants and trees.

Tropical rainforests cover seven per cent of the world's land. They are **home to over half of the world's animals and plants**, which live and thrive side by side. Everything they need is in this amazing bubble of life called **an 'ecosystem'**.

THE AMAZON RAINFOREST

This expedition will take you deep into the **Amazon rainforest**, which covers parts of nine countries in South America including Brazil, Peru and Colombia. It has been around for 55 million years!

The Amazon rainforest is home to one of our planet's most amazing ranges of plants and animals. So get ready for the expedition of a lifetime!

LAYERS OF THE RAINFOREST

The rainforest is made up of four layers. Each layer has different amounts of sunlight and rainfall, so different plants and animals can be found in each one.

EMERGENT LAYER

In the emergent layer, the tops of the **tallest trees rise high into the windy air**. This is the sunniest, rainiest layer in the rainforest. Here, you will find noisy macaws, nesting storks, hunting eagles and soaring vultures.

CANOPY

The canopy is **wet and sunny**. The thick branches and large leaves of taller trees cover the layers below. It is full of fruit and nuts all year and home to more wildlife than any other layer. Here, you will find frogs, monkeys, sloths and more.

UNDERSTOREY

The understorey is the **warm, damp layer, sheltered by the canopy above**. Here, you will find large, shade-loving plants and short trees — the perfect hiding place for climbing wild cats and sleepy plant eaters.

FOREST FLOOR

The forest floor is **the lowest layer** of the rainforest. **It is hot, damp and dark**. Only a tiny bit of sunlight gets through the thick trees and vegetation above. Here, you will find dead leaves, fungi, insects, insect-loving animals, rivers and river wildlife.

YOUR HABITAT MODEL

Your habitat model has three tiers, shown below. **Read the animal profile pages** to discover who lives where in the rainforest and **check out the little diagram** to place the animal models in their correct rainforest home.

Animal models are not to scale.

EMERGENT LAYER

CANOPY

UNDERSTOREY

FOREST FLOOR

WHERE?
Forest floor and understorey

JAGUAR

The jaguar is one of the rainforest's wild cats. This big, powerful predator roams the forest in search of prey.

The jaguar is the **third biggest cat in the world** after the lion and the tiger. It can grow up to 2.5 metres long, from head to tail.

The pattern of the **jaguar's spots acts as camouflage**, helping it to hide easily among the shadows and vegetation.

With its super-strong jaws, powerful bite and piercing canine teeth, **it can bite through a turtle's shell** or a crocodile's skull.

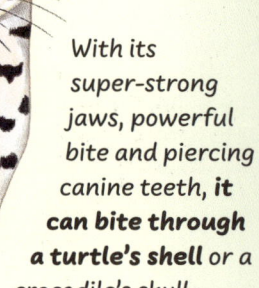

The jaguar is a **good swimmer** and often lives near water. It can climb up into the understorey trees, too.

This powerful big cat is a **top rainforest predator**. It prowls the forest floor hunting for prey including monkeys, lizards and armadillos.

GIANT ANTEATER

The insect-loving giant anteater moves around the forest floor, sniffing out its favourite food.

WHERE?
Forest floor

The giant anteater has a small mouth and no teeth. All the eating work is done with its **long, sticky tongue**, which can reach up to 45 centimetres as it moves in and out to catch tasty insects.

The giant anteater can grow to around **2 metres long**, from the tip of its pointed snout to the end of its bushy tail.

This amazing rainforest animal has **poor eyesight**, but its sense of smell is 40 times more powerful than a human's.

It mostly hunts at night and in the early morning. When it rests, it carves a shallow hole in the ground and **sleeps curled up**.

It uses its powerful front legs and claws to rip open the nests of its **favourite food — ants and termites**.

AMAZON RIVER DOLPHIN

The Amazon river dolphin is a freshwater mammal that can be spotted in the rainforest rivers.

WHERE?
Forest floor rivers

The Amazon river dolphin, also called the **pink river dolphin** or 'boto', hunts for fish, turtles, crabs, shrimp and more.

It is **the most intelligent** of the five living species of river dolphins. Its brain is 40 per cent bigger than the human brain.

It has strong teeth that are like a human's molar teeth — perfect for crunching up food.

The dolphin's flexible body, and its big, paddle-shaped flippers, make it **an excellent swimmer**. It can swim forwards, backwards and upside down.

The Amazon river dolphin is usually found alone, which it likes. Sometimes there are **mother and calf pairs, or small pods (groups)** of three or four.

AMAZONIAN MANATEE

The plant-eating Amazonian manatee is a gentle aquatic mammal with a very big appetite.

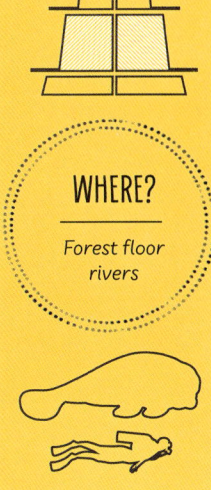

WHERE?

Forest floor rivers

The manatee can grow up to 2.8 metres long and weigh up to 500 kilos. It uses its **big flippers and paddle-like tail** to move through the water.

Although the Amazonian manatee lives in freshwater rivers, it is **also called a 'sea cow'**.

The manatee is a herbivore (plant eater). It can eat up to 8 per cent of its body weight a day and **likes water plants** including water lettuce, water lilies and water hyacinths.

It can **stay underwater for long periods**, coming up to the surface for air every five minutes or so. When it goes down again, its nostrils close to keep water out.

Scientists think that the whiskers around the manatee's snout are **incredible sensors**. Each whisker can tell the difference between textures, which helps the manatee find its favourite seagrasses to eat.

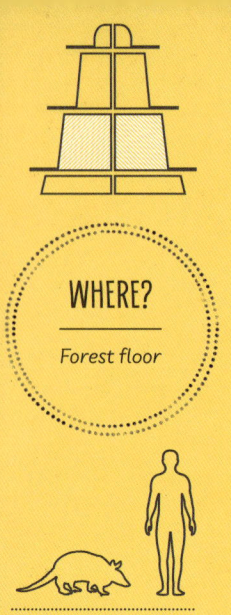

WHERE?
Forest floor

ARMADILLO

The armadillo is an armoured mammal that lives on the forest floor, where it hunts for insects and digs burrows.

Its back, sides, head, legs and tail are mostly protected by **plates of bony armour** — ideal if a hungry jaguar is near. The plates are covered in overlapping scales called 'scutes'.

It has poor eyesight, so it uses its **excellent sense of smell** for searching out food on the rainforest floor.

It has skin pouches on different areas of its body that release a liquid to mark its burrow — **a smelly kind of personal ID** that other armadillos can recognise.

The armadillo uses its **strong, sharp claws** to dig for insects, grubs, small reptiles and fruit. It also uses its claws to dig underground burrows for sleeping, safety and nesting.

This amazing animal is **a good swimmer**. It can cross water by floating on the surface, paddling with its short legs or even holding its breath and walking across the bottom.

HERCULES BEETLE

The Hercules beetle is a giant rainforest insect. It is a species of rhinoceros beetle named after the Greek god Hercules, famous for his strength.

WHERE?
Forest floor and understorey

The Hercules beetle is **one of the largest beetles** in the world. A male can grow up to 19 centimetres long and has huge, pincer-like horns that take up more than half of its size.

In the daytime, the beetle **hides or burrows** in leaf litter on the forest floor.

At night, the Hercules beetle **feeds on fresh and rotting fruit**, vegetation and sometimes other insects and tree sap.

The Hercules beetle may be big and strong, but it still **has enemies**. It is hunted by birds, bats and small mammals.

Males use their **massive horns** to fight each other to win a mate. In battle, they try to lift each other.

BRAZILIAN PORCUPINE

The Brazilian porcupine is a nocturnal, spiky rainforest mammal that spends most of its time in the understorey trees, where it feeds and sleeps.

WHERE?

Forest floor and understorey

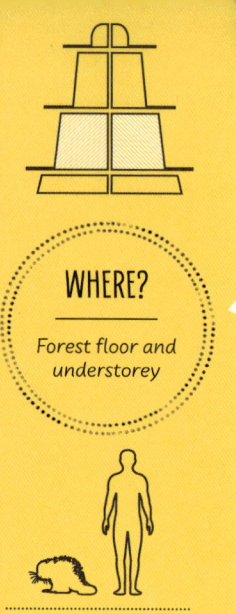

It is covered in **sharp spines, or 'quills'**, that are up to 10 centimetres long and can pierce flesh. Each quill has a hooked 'barb' at the end.

This **plant-eating mammal** likes tree bark, buds, stems, blossoms, fruits, leaves and seeds.

When it is relaxed, the porcupine's quills lie flat, but when it is threatened its **quills stand up straight** in a bold display. The ocelot is its only predator, apart from blood-sucking bugs.

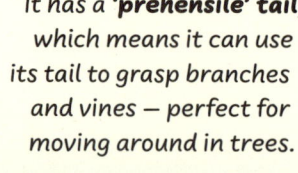

High **forks in branches and hollow trunks** are its favourite places for dens and daytime sleeping. It only comes down to the ground for extra food, to mate, have babies or poo.

It has a **'prehensile' tail**, which means it can use its tail to grasp branches and vines – perfect for moving around in trees.

OCELOT

The ocelot is a sleek, medium-sized rainforest wild cat that comes out at night and during twilight.

WHERE?

Forest floor and understorey

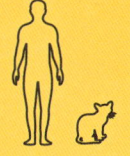

The ocelot lives in areas with **plenty of prey** to hunt and water to drink. It keeps away from other predators and jumps into trees to escape them.

In the daytime, the ocelot **rests in trees**, or in cool, sheltered dens on the forest floor.

The ocelot is excellent at climbing and leaping. It **likes water** and is a good swimmer.

Like the jaguar, the ocelot's **rosette-like markings** help it to hide in the light and shade of the rainforest plants and trees.

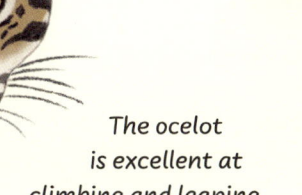

At night, it hunts for prey including armadillos, small mammals, fish, insects, reptiles and birds.

BLACK CAIMAN

WHERE?
Forest floor rivers

The black caiman is a large semiaquatic reptile with dark, scaly skin. It is a top predator and can grow to around 4.5 metres from tail to snout.

It **lives along riverbanks**, streams and areas with plenty of dense vegetation and lots of prey.

Its **eyes and nose** are on top of its head, so it can see and breathe while the rest of it is underwater.

Its **big jaws can gape wide** to snatch prey, chomping down with a bite powerful enough to shatter a turtle's shell.

Female caimans **build nest mounds** where they lay 30 to 60 eggs at a time. Not all of these will hatch to produce babies called 'hatchlings'.

A top Amazon predator, the black caiman **mostly hunts at night**. Prey includes tapirs, pythons, Amazon river dolphins, monkeys and sloths.

TAPIR

The Amazon rainforest tapir is a shy mammal. It forages for vegetation and fruit at night and rests or hides in the daytime.

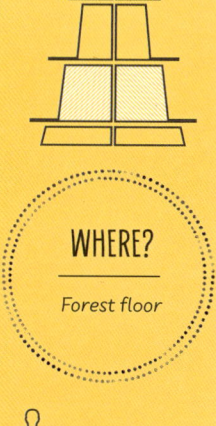

WHERE?

Forest floor

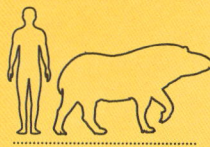

This tapir can grow up to 2 metres long and is the **size of a small pony**. It is the Amazon's largest surviving native land mammal, which means it has always lived there.

The tapir has hooves and a **stand-up mane** that runs from its forehead to its shoulders.

It is a **strong swimmer** and likes to live near water, especially rivers. If it is alarmed by a predator, it heads for the water to escape.

It likes to forage for food at night and uses its **flexible snout, or 'proboscis'**, to grab hold of leaves and fruit. It has large teeth, perfect for grinding up seeds and plants.

Adult tapirs are reddish-brown, but their **babies have a striped coat** for camouflage. The pattern fades when they are around 7 months old.

EMERALD TREE BOA

The emerald tree boa spends most of the time high up in the leafy rainforest canopy. It is a night-time hunter that lies in wait for prey.

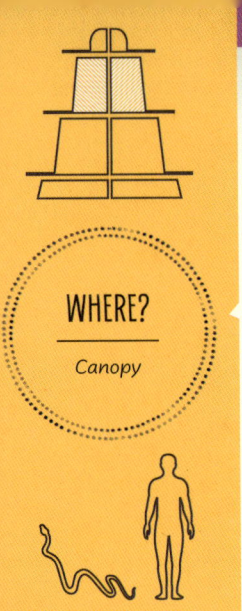

WHERE?
Canopy

This **2-metre-long** snake has a 'prehensile' tail that it uses to hold onto branches, so it can dangle down among the vegetation.

It has **large heat sensors** around its mouth. These can detect the heat from nearby prey.

Unlike most snakes, the emerald tree boa doesn't lay eggs (eggs hatch inside the mother), but **gives birth to live baby snakes**.

Its distinctive bright-green colour with white markings is **great camouflage**, making it tricky for unsuspecting prey to spot it.

The snake lies in wait to ambush rodents and other small mammals. It attacks by biting prey with its sharp front teeth, then it **coils itself tightly** around it to squeeze and kill it.

EMPEROR TAMARIN

The emperor tamarin is a small, energetic, friendly and playful kind of monkey that lives in the rainforest canopy. Its nickname is 'moustache monkey'.

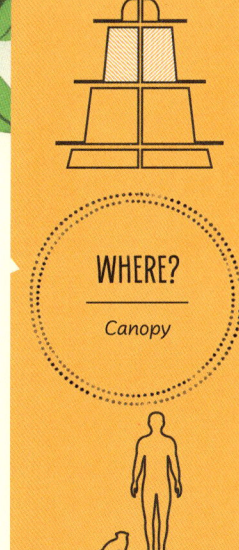

WHERE?
Canopy

The emperor tamarin is **playful and sociable**, living in groups of up to 15. Tamarins communicate with different calls to tell each other about friends, enemies and strangers in their territory.

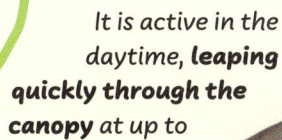

It is active in the daytime, **leaping quickly through the canopy** at up to 40 kilometres per hour. It clings to trees with its claws and hardly ever touches the forest floor.

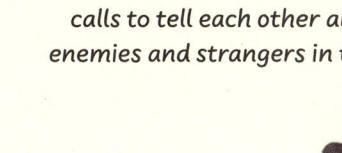

With a body length of around **26 centimetres**, this small mammal is easy prey for predators including wild cats, snakes and birds of prey.

Emperor tamarins are 'social groomers', which means that they **groom each other** as a way of strengthening the bonds between them.

The tamarin is an 'omnivore', which means it **eats plants and animals**. It mostly feeds on fruit, but it also eats insects, plant gum, flowers, nectar, leaves, frogs, snails and even small birds.

SQUIRREL MONKEY

The squirrel monkey lives in large groups in the rainforest canopy, running and jumping through the leafy trees.

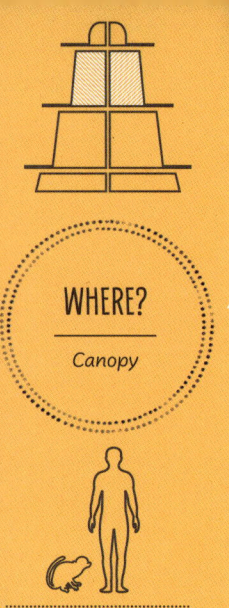

WHERE?
Canopy

Squirrel monkeys **live in huge troops** of up to 500 members. They communicate with calls including barks, peeps, purrs, squawks and screams.

The monkey uses its **long tail to help it balance** as it leaps around the canopy.

In the day, squirrel monkeys hunt for insects and fruits to eat. **At night, they huddle together** on branches to sleep.

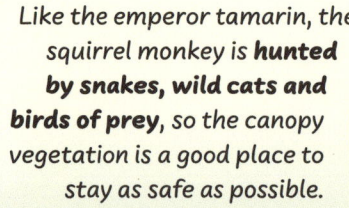

The monkey's rainforest home is hot and damp. One of the ways it cools itself is to **urinate (wee) on its hands** and rub the urine (wee) on the soles of its feet. As the urine dries, this cools it down.

Like the emperor tamarin, the squirrel monkey is **hunted by snakes, wild cats and birds of prey**, so the canopy vegetation is a good place to stay as safe as possible.

RED-EYED TREE FROG

The red-eyed tree frog lives in the hot, damp rainforest canopy, where it clings to leaves and hunts for insects.

WHERE?
Canopy

This tree frog is famous for its **bright-green body**, colourful markings, bright-orange feet and red eyes.

In the day, its green colouring helps it to hide from danger, camouflaged among the leafy plants and trees. If it is disturbed, a **flash of its red eyes** can help to startle predators.

Females **lay up to 40 eggs** on the undersides of leaves, over water. When the tadpoles hatch out, they drop down into the water, where they stay for weeks until they develop into froglets.

It is nocturnal and **spends the night hunting** for insects including moths, crickets, flies and grasshoppers.

Its **webbed feet have suction cups** which help it to cling easily to leaves, high above the ground.

GREEN IGUANA

The green iguana is a large, plant-eating lizard that lives in the canopy trees and grows to around 1.75 metres long from head to black-striped tail.

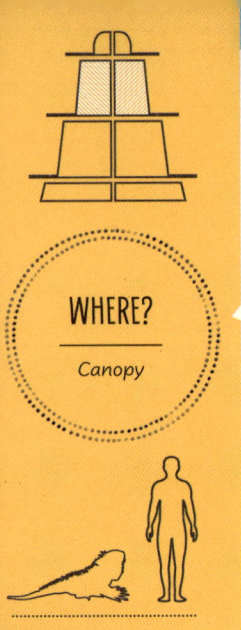

WHERE?
Canopy

It has a **sensory organ on top of its head** which can detect movement and changes in light, telling it if danger is near.

It only **climbs down from the canopy occasionally** — to mate, lay eggs, or to make its way to a different tree.

The green iguana's **teeth are broad, flat and serrated** on the edge, similar to those of its dinosaur relations. They are excellent for shredding leaves.

It can use its **tail like a powerful whip** to strike attackers, but if its tail is grabbed, the iguana allows it to break off. This means the iguana can escape and eventually a new tail grows.

A **row of spines along its back and tail** help to protect it from predators, but if it is cornered, it extends the red flap under its neck, called a 'dewlap'. It also puffs up its body, bobs its head and hisses in a bold defence display.

HOWLER MONKEY

The noisy howler monkey lives in the canopy trees, where its loud howls can be heard up to 5 kilometres away.

WHERE?
Canopy

The howler monkey is the **loudest land animal**. Males have a large throat and a special vocal chamber, so can make extremely loud calls at dawn and dusk to protect their territory.

The monkey's **short snout has lots of sensory hairs** inside, which help to pick up the smell of food up to 2 kilometres away.

It moves along high canopy branches on **all four legs**, searching out rainforest fruit, nuts and leaves to eat.

The howler monkey grows to around 70 centimetres long, not including its long 'prehensile' tail, which it uses for **grasping branches**.

Howler monkeys **live in troops** of as many as 15 monkeys, with up to three adult males and lots of females.

TWO-TOED SLOTH

The two-toed sloth is famous for being a very slow mover. It spends most of its life hanging upside down in the canopy.

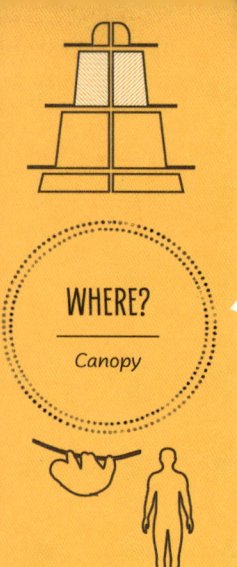

WHERE?
Canopy

The two-toed sloth gets its name from the **two curved toes** on its front feet.

It has specially-adapted bones and muscles, so it can **hang onto branches safely**, hour after hour.

Its body can store very large amounts of poo and wee, so it only **goes down to the ground about once a week** to defecate (poo and wee).

Its **long, shaggy fur** often has green algae (tiny living organisms) growing in it, which can help the sloth stay camouflaged from predators, among the vegetation.

With a **top speed of a quarter of a kilometre an hour** and poor eyesight, the sloth is in danger from rainforest predators including jaguars, ocelots and harpy eagles.

TOCO TOUCAN

The toco toucan is a striking rainforest bird with glossy black feathers and a large, brightly-coloured bill (beak).

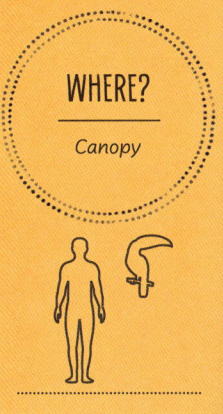

WHERE?
Canopy

The toco toucan is **the biggest kind of toucan**. It is very sociable and lives in pairs, or flocks of up to six birds.

It **feeds on fruit and nuts** that grow in the canopy, but it sometimes goes down to the ground in search of fallen fruits.

The toco toucan **isn't built for long flights**. Instead, it flies in short bursts, or glides.

Its **23-centimetre-long** bill is hollow and light, with serrated (jagged) edges — perfect for plucking fruit to eat. It also acts as a radiator that releases heat from the bird's body to keep it cool.

The toucan **adds to its fruit-and-nut diet** by eating insects, small reptiles, frogs and the eggs of other birds.

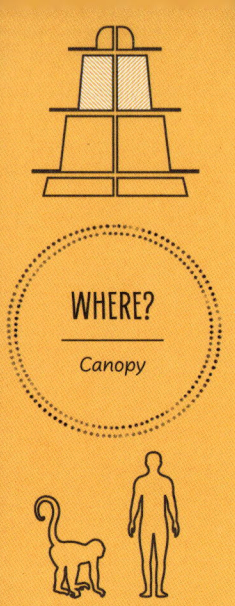

WHERE?
Canopy

BLACK SPIDER MONKEY

The black spider monkey swings through the canopy and plays an important part in helping new rainforest plants to grow.

Its **long, spider-like limbs** and long, gripping tail help it to move easily through the trees.

A **baby black spider monkey** is carried on its mother's tummy for the first four months of its life, before moving onto her back.

Black spider monkeys live in **troops of around 30**, feeding in the morning and resting in the afternoon.

It **is omnivorous**, which means it eats a range of food including fruits, nuts, buds, insects, flowers and eggs.

As the spider monkey moves around, it does the important job of **spreading seeds that it leaves behind** in its poo. These seeds grow into new rainforest plants and trees.

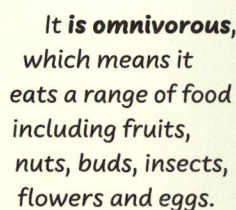

AMAZONIAN UMBRELLABIRD

The Amazonian umbrellabird is a secretive canopy bird with a love of fruit and nuts. The males make loud, booming calls.

WHERE?
Canopy

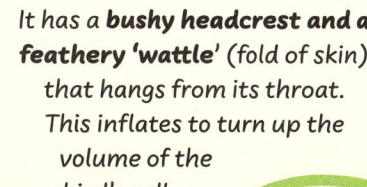

The umbrellabird flies across openings in the rainforest trees in an **up-and-down movement**.

It has a **bushy headcrest and a feathery 'wattle'** (fold of skin) that hangs from its throat. This inflates to turn up the volume of the bird's call.

The umbrellabird **forages alone or in small groups**. It searches for fruit and berries, plus spiders and large insects if it can find them.

In the trees, the umbrellabird **hops from branch to branch** with the help of its clawed toes.

Males gather in groups called 'leks', where they inflate their wattles and call to attract females.

WHITE-TAILED HAWK

The white-tailed hawk is a large, powerful bird of prey that perches in treetops and hovers in mid-air as it searches for its next meal.

WHERE?
Emergent layer

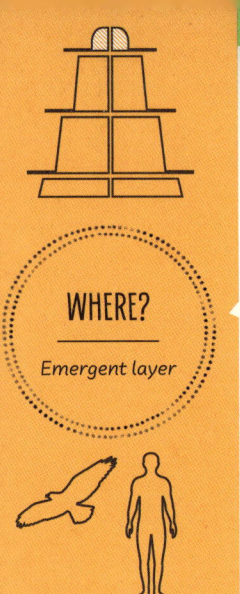

It has a **wingspan of almost 1.5 metres** from tip to tip. In flight, it leans into the wind and flaps its wings just enough so it can hover in mid-air, over the same spot.

Like all hawks, it has **incredible eyesight** and can spot far-off prey from great heights. It hunts for creatures including rats, lizards, snakes, frogs, insects and even dead animals.

A male and female pair build a nest from broken twigs and line it with dried grasses, ready for laying eggs. The pair **return to the same nest every year** and make it bigger.

The white-tailed hawk makes **a high-pitched call** that almost sounds like a cackle. It uses this alarm sound if it spies an intruder in its territory, or approaching its nest.

Its feet have **sharp, curved talons** for catching prey and a strong, hooked beak for biting and tearing flesh.

JABIRU STORK

The huge jabiru stork builds a nest platform in the tallest treetops and fishes for food in the water far down below.

WHERE?
Emergent layer

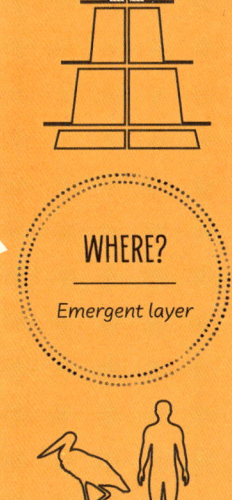

It **catches fish in its open bill**, then throws its head back to swallow them down. It also eats frogs, insects, snakes and other small creatures, and even feeds on dead animals.

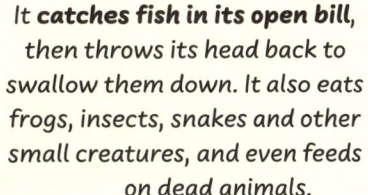

The jabiru stork can grow to 1.5 metres high and is **the tallest flying bird** in South America. Its long legs are perfect for wading in shallow water to hunt for fish.

It has a **red throat sac**, or pouch, that inflates when it is excited.

Jabiru storks greet each other by **clattering their bills loudly**, waving their necks from side to side and moving their heads up and down.

A pair of male and female jabiru storks **build a massive nest platform** of sticks in a high tree above the rainforest. They use it year after year.

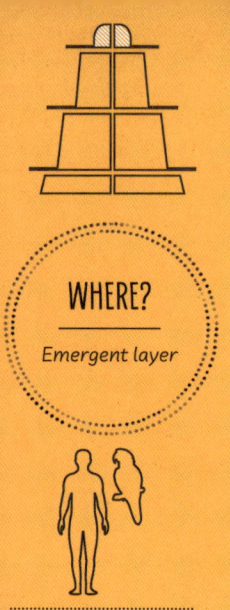

WHERE?
Emergent layer

SCARLET MACAW

The scarlet macaw is one of the most colourful birds in the Amazon rainforest — and one of the noisiest.

Scarlet macaws **make their nests in tree hollows** high up in the rainforest's emergent layer.

These birds **feed in large, noisy groups**, eating the fruits, seeds, flowers and nuts that grow in their forest home. They like bugs and snails, too.

A mating pair of scarlet macaws **stay together for life**. The birds preen and lick each other's faces.

The macaw **grips food with its clawed feet** and holds it up to its powerful beak to crush and eat.

Macaws **communicate with very loud squawks**, squeaks and even screams that carry for kilometres through the rainforest.

KING VULTURE

The large, powerful king vulture lives high up in the branches of the rainforest's emergent layer and can soar for hours in the warm air.

WHERE?
Emergent layer

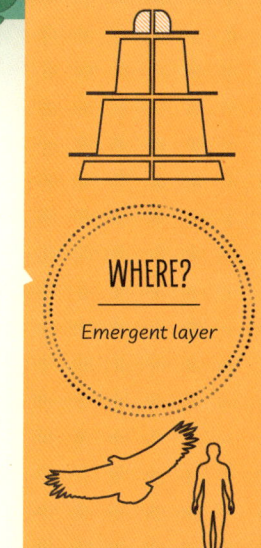

Like other vultures, **the king vulture is a scavenger**, which means it does not kill its own food. It feeds on the bodies and remains of dead animals, called 'carrion'.

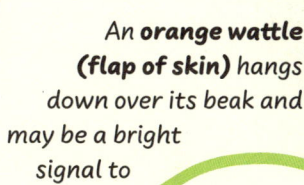

The king vulture has **excellent eyesight** and can easily spot a dead animal from its treetop perch. If it sees another vulture eating a carcass, it shoots down to push it out of the way.

An **orange wattle (flap of skin)** hangs down over its beak and may be a bright signal to attract a mate.

It uses its thick, **strong beak to rip the skin of a carcass** and shred flesh. Its strong claws grip hold of its meal which might be a large mammal, a monkey, a fish or a lizard. It isn't a fussy eater.

The king vulture's **only predators are snakes — and jaguars**, if they manage to surprise the bird while it is eating.

HARPY EAGLE

The harpy eagle is one of the world's largest, most powerful eagles. It is a top rainforest predator and hunts big mammals.

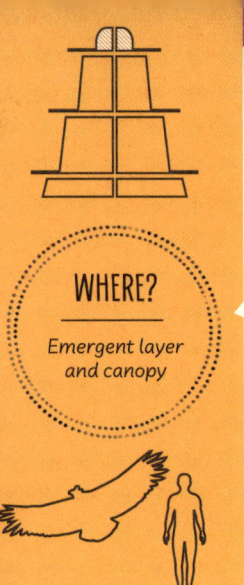

WHERE?

Emergent layer and canopy

The harpy eagle **hunts for sloths, monkeys and other canopy mammals**. It does not hunt daily, as it can feed on the same dead prey for a few days, even when it is slightly rotten.

It has **excellent eyesight and hearing** to help it detect prey in the dark, green rainforest vegetation.

Its **killing talons are up to 10 centimetres** long and have an immensely strong grip.

It has a **disk of feathers around its face**, like an owl's. The feathers can be raised to direct sounds to the bird's ears.

Male and female pairs **build a nest high in the tallest trees** and raise their chicks together. Young harpy eagles depend on their parents until they are two years old.

QUICK QUIZ

What can you remember from your rainforest expedition? Try answering these quick-fire questions to see if you have achieved 'expert' level.

Which rainforest beetle can grow up to 19 centimetres long?

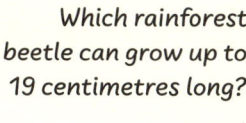

Which spiky rainforest mammal has a 'prehensile' tail?

Which rainforest reptile can crush a turtle's shell with its powerful bite?

Which tree-dweller has red eyes that can startle predators?

Which noisy monkey can be heard up to 5 kilometres away?

Who moves at a top speed of a quarter of a kilometre an hour?

Which bird is famous for its colourful feathers and noisy nature?

USEFUL WORDS

These are a few of the words that are useful for a rainforest explorer to know.

Algae: tiny, simple living organisms, usually small plants

Camouflage: the way an animal's shape, colour or pattern helps it to blend in with its surroundings

Carrion: dead or decaying flesh

Ecosystem: an area where all living things work together in a bubble of life, side by side

Herbivore: an animal that only eats plants

Mammal: any animal where the female feeds her young on her own milk

Nocturnal: being active at night, not in the day

Omnivore: an animal that eats both plants and meat (living things)

Predator: an animal that hunts, kills and eats other animals

Prehensile: a part of the body able to hold things, especially by curling around them, or gripping

Proboscis: the long nose or snout of some animals

Reptile: a cold-blooded animal that produces eggs and uses the sun's heat to keep its blood warm

Scavenger: a bird or animal that feeds on dead animals that it has not killed itself

Semiaquatic: living partly on land and partly in the water

Species: a set of similar animals or plants, that can breed with each other

Wattle: the loose fold of skin that hangs from a bird's neck